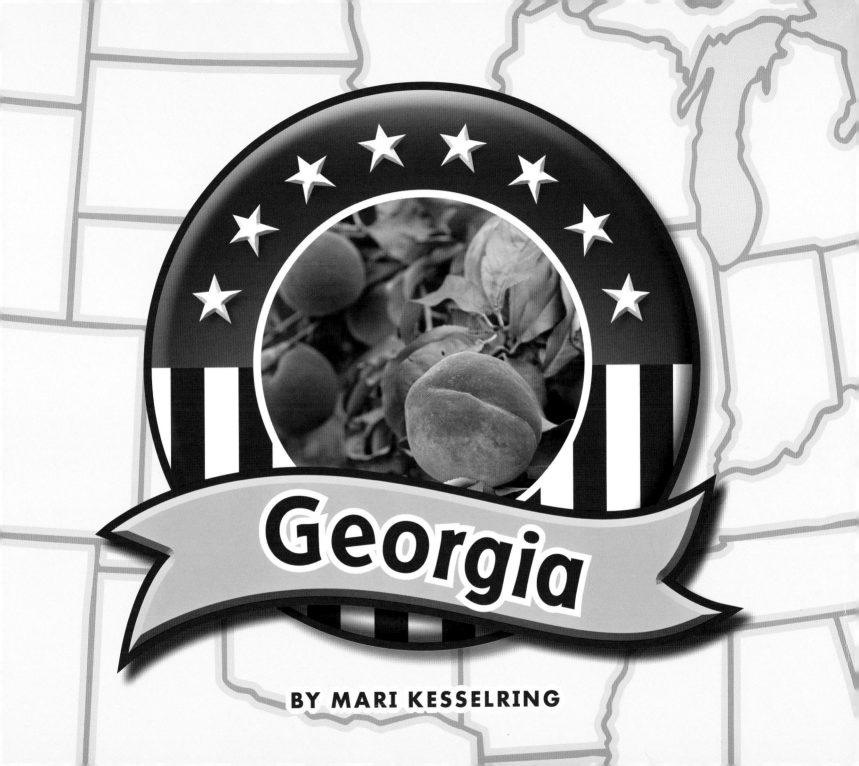

Georgia

BY MARI KESSELRING

Published by The Child's World®
1980 Lookout Drive • Mankato, MN 56003-1705
800-599-READ • www.childsworld.com

ACKNOWLEDGMENTS
The Child's World®: Mary Berendes, Publishing Director
The Design Lab: Design and production
Red Line Editorial: Editorial direction

PHOTO CREDITS: P.M. Augustavo Photography/iStockphoto, cover, 1, 3;
Matt Kania/Map Hero, Inc., 4, 5; Jeremy Edwards/iStockphoto, 7; Sebastien
Windal/iStockphoto, 9; iStockphoto, 10; Alan Tobey/iStockphoto, 11; Seth
Perlman/AP Images, 13; North Wind Pictures/Photolibrary, 15; Barbara
Kraus/iStockphoto, 17; AP Images, 19; Greg Henry/Shutterstock Images, 21;
One Mile Up, 22; Quarter-dollar coin image from the United States Mint, 22

LIBRARY OF CONGRESS CATALOGING-IN-PUBLICATION DATA
Kesselring, Mari.
  Georgia / by Mari Kesselring.
    p. cm.
  Includes bibliographical references and index.
  ISBN 978-1-60253-454-4 (library bound : alk. paper)
  1. Georgia—Juvenile literature. I. Title.

F286.3.K47 2010
975.8—dc22

                                      2010017673

Printed in the United States of America in Mankato, Minnesota.
May 2012
PA02138

On the cover:
Georgia is called
"the Peach State."

CONTENTS

Geography

Let's explore Georgia! Georgia is in the southeastern United States. The Atlantic Ocean is to the east.

TENNESSEE

NORTH CAROLINA

Dalton •

Blue Ridge
Mountains

Cartersville •

SOUTH CAROLINA

Stone
Mountain

• Athens

Atlanta ★

NORTH

WEST   EAST

SOUTH

Augusta •

ALABAMA

• Macon

Dublin •

• Columbus

Plains •

GEORGIA

Savannah •

Albany •

Atlantic
Ocean

Valdosta •

FLORIDA

Cities

Atlanta is the capital of Georgia. It is also the largest city in the state. Augusta, Columbus, and Savannah are other large cities in Georgia.

Atlanta is one of the biggest cities in the United States. ▶

Land

Northern Georgia has some mountains. The Blue Ridge Mountains are the highest mountains in the state. Valleys are between the mountains. Georgia also has some flat land that is used for farming. Beaches are along the ocean.

Forests cover much of Georgia's mountains. ▶

Plants and Animals

Forests cover more than half of Georgia. The state tree is the live oak. It is a common tree in the South. The Georgia state bird is the brown thrasher. This bird can be almost a foot (.3 m) long. It has a rounded beak. The state flower is the Cherokee rose. It is a white flower with a **thorny** stem.

Live oaks can be found throughout Georgia. ▶

The Cherokee rose is named for the Cherokee, a Native American tribe. They are an important part of Georgia's history.

People and Work

More than 9 million people live in Georgia. Many people work in jobs that help other people. Some are government jobs. Other people work in **manufacturing** or farming. Many Georgia farmers grow peaches.

A peach grower picks the peaches that are ready to eat. ▶

History

Native Americans have lived in the Georgia area for more than 10,000 years. Georgia became a **colony** owned by England in 1732. It was the last English colony formed in the United States. Georgia became the fourth state on January 2, 1788. During the U.S. **Civil War**, Georgia was one of the first states to join the **Confederate States of America**.

Georgians fought for the Confederate States of America during the Civil War. ▶

Georgia was named after England's King George II.

15

Ways of Life

Many people in Georgia enjoy the arts. These include dancing and painting. People in the state also enjoy outdoor activities such as **surfing**, **hiking**, and mountain climbing.

Jekyll Island Beach in Georgia is a nice place to visit. ▶

Famous People

Civil rights leader Martin Luther King Jr. was born in Atlanta. Musicians Ray Charles and Little Richard were also born in Georgia. Writer Alice Walker was born in the state, too. She wrote the book *The Color Purple*. It won an important award.

After Martin Luther King Jr.'s death, the U.S. government made a national holiday in his honor. ▶

Famous Places

Stone Mountain is a **popular** place to visit. The faces of men who helped the South fight the Civil War are carved into the rock. They are Robert E. Lee, Jefferson Davis, and Stonewall Jackson. Visitors also enjoy **museums**.

Stone Mountain is the largest **formation** of **granite** in North America. ▶

State Symbols

Seal

The date 1776 on the Georgia state seal is when the United States was formed. Go to childsworld.com/links for a link to Georgia's state Web site, where you can get a firsthand look at the state seal.

Flag

Georgia's state flag has 13 stars because Georgia was one of the first 13 colonies.

Quarter

Georgia's state quarter shows the peach, the state fruit. The oak leaves stand for the Georgia state tree. The quarter came out in 1999.

Glossary

civil rights (SIV-il RITES): Civil rights are the rights every human should have. Martin Luther King Jr., who was born in Georgia, was a civil rights leader.

Civil War (SIV-il WOR): In the United States, the Civil War was a war fought between the Northern and the Southern states from 1861 to 1865. People from Georgia fought for the South in the Civil War.

colony (KOL-uh-nee): A colony is an area of land that is newly settled and is controlled by a government of another land. Georgia was once a colony owned by England.

Confederate States of America (kun-FED-ur-ut STAYTS UHV uh-MAYR-uh-kuh): The Confederate States of America was the group of 11 states that left the United States to form their own nation during the U.S. Civil War. Georgia was part of the Confederate States of America.

formation (for-MAY-shun): A formation is a shape of something. Stone Mountain is a rock formation in Georgia.

granite (GRAN-it): Granite is a type of hard rock. Stone Mountain is made of granite.

hiking (HYK-ing): Hiking is taking a walk in a natural area, such as a hill or a mountain. People enjoy hiking in Georgia.

manufacturing (man-yuh-FAK-chur-ing): Manufacturing is the task of making items with machines. Some people in Georgia work in manufacturing.

museums (myoo-ZEE-umz): Museums are places where people go to see art, history, or science displays. Georgia has several museums.

popular (POP-yuh-lur): To be popular is to be enjoyed by many people. Stone Mountain is a popular place to visit in Georgia.

seal (SEEL): A seal is a symbol a state uses for government business. The year on the Georgia seal is when the United States was formed.

surfing (SURF-ing): Surfing is riding big waves on a long board. People in Georgia enjoy surfing on the Atlantic Ocean.

symbols (SIM-bulz): Symbols are pictures or things that stand for something else. The flag and seal are Georgia's symbols.

thorny (THORN-ee): Something that is thorny is covered with sharp points. The stem of the Cherokee rose, Georgia's state flower, is thorny.

tribe (TRYB): A tribe is a group of people who share ancestors and customs. The Cherokee has been an important Native American tribe in Georgia.

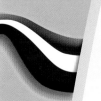

Further Information

Books

Bredeson, Carmen. *Georgia*. New York: Children's Press, 2003.

Crane, Carol. *P is for Peach: A Georgia Alphabet*. Chelsea, MI: Sleeping Bear Press, 2002.

Sullivan, E. J. *G is for Georgia*. Raleigh, NC: Sweetwater Press, 2006.

Web Sites

Visit our Web site for links about Georgia: *childsworld.com/links*

Note to Parents, Teachers, and Librarians: We routinely verify our Web links to make sure they are safe and active sites. So encourage your readers to check them out!

Index